Villains All

Compiled by Pat Edwards and Wendy Body

Acknowlegements

We are grateful to the following for permission to reproduce copyright material: the author, Paul Groves for his poem 'Superchoppers'; New Zealand Department of Education for the story 'The New House Villain' from *School Journal* by Margaret Mahy © 1977 Margaret Mahy; Penguin Books Australia Ltd for 'Brian' from *In the Garden of Badthings* by Doug MacLeod; Scholastic-TAB Publications for the story 'The Bicycle Thieves' from *The Kids From B.A.D.* by Allen Morgan © 1984 Allen Morgan. Pages 24-5 and 42-3 were written by Debbie Fox. We are grateful to Mr. C. Downing at the Transport and Road Research Laboratory, ROSPA, and the Road Safety Unit at Hertfordshire County Council for their advice.

We have been unable to trace the copyright holder in the song 'Mr Wobblegoose's Bicycle' by Kenneth Anderson and would appreciate any information that would enable us to do so.

We are grateful to the following for permission to reproduce photographs: All Sport, page 43 below left; Northumberland Tourist Board, pages 42-3 (background), 42 centre, 42 below, 43 above right and centre right; ROSPA, page 25; Tyne & Wear Museums Service, pages 42 above, 43 below centre and below right.

Illustrators include: Rolf Heimann pp. 4-5, 62-3; Andrew Reid pp. 6-21; Bob Shields pp. 22-3, 60-1, Maggie Ling pp. 24-5; Alan Jane pp. 26-8; Peter Solomon pp. 29-38; Edward McLachlan pp. 46-57; Marjorie Gardner pp. 58-9; Kathy Baxendale p. 64.

Contents

Jailhouse jokes   4
The Bicycle Thieves   *Allen Morgan*   6
Mr Wobblegoose's Bicycle   *Kenneth Anderson*   22
Don't be a wobblegoose   24
Wheeling through time   26
The New House Villain   *Margaret Mahy*   28
Brian   *Doug MacLeod*   39
Meet a writer: Margaret Mahy   40
It's my home: Newcastle   42
What's up, Sir Edmund?   44
Superchoppers   *Paul Groves*   46
Pages from the notebook of Private Eye Sally Snooper   58
How does it work? The telephone   60
Catch a crook!   62
Words to track down   *Glossary*   63

THE BICYCLE THIEVES

from *The Kids From B.A.D.*

When John's brand new BMX racer
is stolen, he decides he isn't going to take
the loss lying down, so he and his friends form the
Barton Avenue Detectives — alias The Kids from B.A.D.
They decide to search the neighbourhood for clues. At first they
have little success, but . . .

John and Sally were on foot patrol a few blocks from John's house when Sally spotted the blue van again, cruising down the street.

"There they are!" she cried, grabbing John's arm.

"After them!" John answered, and they took off in pursuit.

The van was going very slowly so John and Sally had no difficulty catching up. When it stopped at the kerb about halfway down the block, they hid behind a tree.

"Write down the registration number," whispered John. "I'm going to sneak closer and get a good look at what they're up to."

He crept along behind some parked cars until he was right across the street from the van. He could see two men inside. The driver was pointing to a bicycle on a nearby porch as the second man wrote something down in a book. Then they both laughed and the van pulled away from the kerb and started down the street.

"It's them all right," John told Sally when she joined him again. "They're planning another hit. Let's keep them in sight."

John and Sally followed the van as it drove slowly around the block. But just when they figured they had the case all sewn up, they ran into more trouble. The van turned back onto a main street and pulled out into heavy traffic.

"Hey, they're getting away," cried John. "We have to stop them."

"We've got their registration number," Sally said. "We can just report that to the police."

"But it might not do us any good," John explained. "What if they stole that van they're driving? Then the registration number wouldn't help the police trace them. The only sure way to find their hideout is to follow them ourselves." He started running down the footpath.

"We'll never catch them running," Sally shouted after him, but then she saw that that wasn't the idea at all. John had stopped part way down the block where a taxicab was parked. He waved for Sally to join him, then climbed in. When she got there he pulled her inside too.

"Follow that van!" he told the cabby breathlessly.

The cab driver turned around and stared at him. "You've got to be kidding," he said.

"He's not," said Sally. "Hurry, we don't want to lose them!"

"I've been driving this cab fifteen years now," said the cabby, "and not once has anyone ever told me to 'follow that car'."

"Van," insisted Sally. "Come on, it's getting away."

"You kids have been watching too much TV," the cabby continued. "Let's go. Out of the cab now and no fooling around. I'm working."

"But we can pay," John explained, pulling out the twenty-dollar bill his grandmother had given him. He knew the time had come to use it.

The cabby looked at it for a moment. Then he shrugged. "Your money, your cab," he said and turned on the motor, muttering to himself, "Fifteen years and I thought I'd heard everything. 'Follow that car.' Who'd believe it?"

He started his meter and pulled out into the street. Sally and John grew restless as the blue van continued to pull farther and farther ahead of them. But the cabby didn't seem very concerned about staying close behind.

"You two seem a little young for cops," he said conversationally.

"We're detectives," explained John. "I'm the chief."

"And I'm the assistant chief," said Sally.

"And *I'm* the Minister of Transport," said the cabby, chuckling to himself. "I bet that van's full of money from a bank hold-up, right? Or maybe it's just a simple kidnapping case?"

"Stolen bicycles," said John, and he went on to explain the case.

"Stolen bike ring, eh?" said the cabby, suddenly serious again. "Sounds like you might have something — my boy just had his bike taken two weeks ago. You think these guys had something to do with it?"

After that the cabby gave all his attention to staying right on the tail of the blue van. He almost lost it a few times in the heavy traffic, but he was right behind it when it turned into a driveway on the other side of town. He pulled over to the kerb half a block farther on.

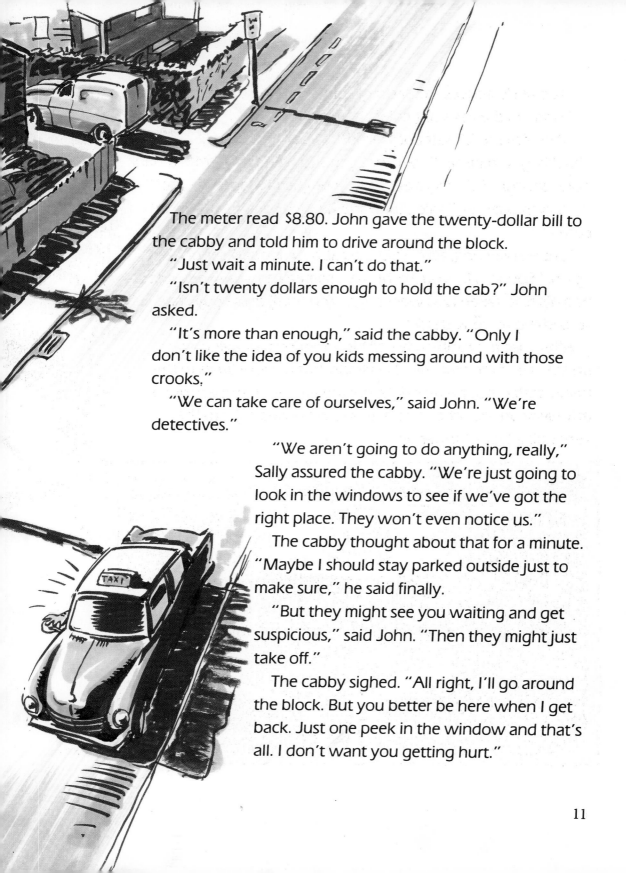

The meter read $8.80. John gave the twenty-dollar bill to the cabby and told him to drive around the block.

"Just wait a minute. I can't do that."

"Isn't twenty dollars enough to hold the cab?" John asked.

"It's more than enough," said the cabby. "Only I don't like the idea of you kids messing around with those crooks."

"We can take care of ourselves," said John. "We're detectives."

"We aren't going to do anything, really," Sally assured the cabby. "We're just going to look in the windows to see if we've got the right place. They won't even notice us."

The cabby thought about that for a minute. "Maybe I should stay parked outside just to make sure," he said finally.

"But they might see you waiting and get suspicious," said John. "Then they might just take off."

The cabby sighed. "All right, I'll go around the block. But you better be here when I get back. Just one peek in the window and that's all. I don't want you getting hurt."

John and Sally climbed out of the cab and started back down the block as the cabby drove slowly in the other direction. They crept along the side of the house and peeked around the corner. Through the back window they could see the two men drinking beer at a kitchen table as they studied a city street map. The smaller of the two traced a path down the map with his finger while the other made notes in a small book.

Sally and John went part way back down the driveway, then stopped to talk.

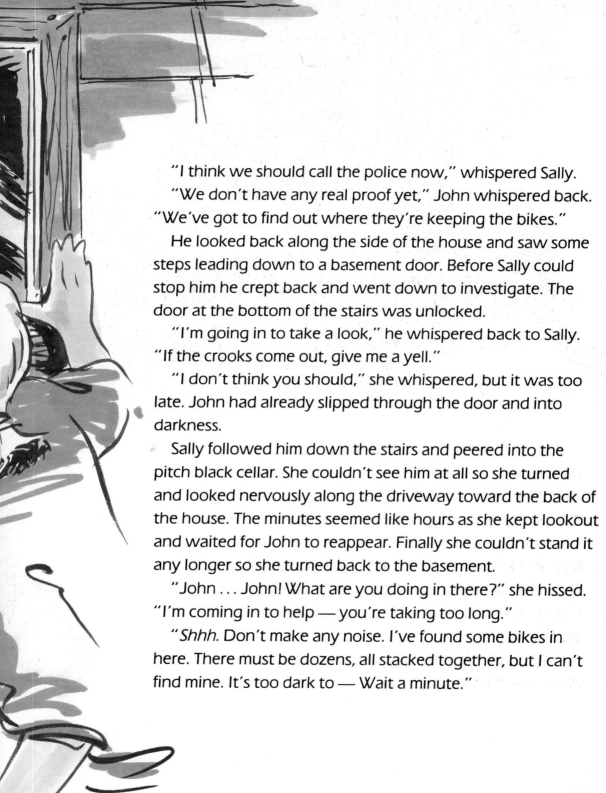

"I think we should call the police now," whispered Sally.

"We don't have any real proof yet," John whispered back. "We've got to find out where they're keeping the bikes."

He looked back along the side of the house and saw some steps leading down to a basement door. Before Sally could stop him he crept back and went down to investigate. The door at the bottom of the stairs was unlocked.

"I'm going in to take a look," he whispered back to Sally. "If the crooks come out, give me a yell."

"I don't think you should," she whispered, but it was too late. John had already slipped through the door and into darkness.

Sally followed him down the stairs and peered into the pitch black cellar. She couldn't see him at all so she turned and looked nervously along the driveway toward the back of the house. The minutes seemed like hours as she kept lookout and waited for John to reappear. Finally she couldn't stand it any longer so she turned back to the basement.

"John . . . John! What are you doing in there?" she hissed. "I'm coming in to help — you're taking too long."

"*Shhh*. Don't make any noise. I've found some bikes in here. There must be dozens, all stacked together, but I can't find mine. It's too dark to — Wait a minute."

13

There was a moment of silence, then suddenly a great crash sounded in the darkness. Sally gasped.

"John! What happened? Are you all right?"

The basement lights snapped on and Sally could see John in the middle of a heap of fallen bicycles. Then she heard footsteps at the top of the inside stairs. She ran to John and tried to pull him clear of the bicycles but it was too late. The two men were coming down the stairs.

"What's going on here?" asked the short man angrily. He went over to John, but John hardly noticed him.

"I found it!" he cried triumphantly at Sally.

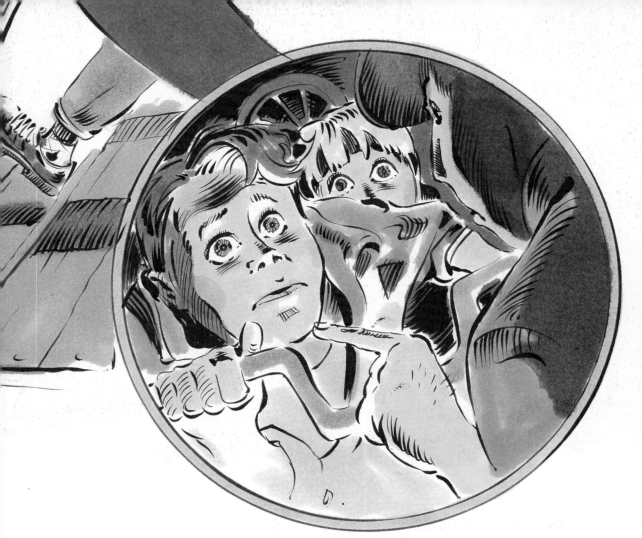

"Found what?" demanded the short man.

"My bike. The one that was . . ." John's voice trailed off as
he realised what he'd almost said.

The bigger man swore under his breath. The short one
licked his lips nervously.

"You're making a mistake here, kid," he said. "We just got
these bikes second-hand from a guy we know. That one's
probably just the same colour as yours."

"Maybe you're right," John said quickly. "Listen, it
probably just looks like my bike."

The two men looked at each other for a long moment, then the short one turned back to John. "You and the girl just sit tight for a minute while me and my partner have a little discussion here." He went back over to the big man and started talking to him quietly.

Sally helped John to his feet. "We're going to have to do something," she whispered.

John nodded. "Looks like trouble, all right."

"I've got a plan," Sally said. "You get them talking so they won't be watching me. I'll sneak over to the door. When I get a chance, I'll make a break for it and go for the police."

John didn't get a chance to answer her because the two men finished talking and the short one turned back to him again.

"Listen, kid," he said. "If you say that's your bike then I guess we believe you. Me and my partner think maybe this second-hand guy has something crooked going with the bikes he's been selling us, so we're going to report him to the police as soon as we can. But we were thinking, in the meantime why don't you just take your bike back home? We'll let you have it right now, and if you get out of here fast we won't tell the police about you two breaking in here. Ain't that right, Bill?"

The other man grunted but didn't smile. John knew the men were lying but he decided it might be a good idea to play along. If the two crooks were stupid enough to let them go, it would be safer than making a run for it. He'd get his bike back for sure, and he and Sally could still go straight to the police.

"Sounds fair to me," he said finally.

The short man looked relieved. He grinned at his partner. "See, I told you he'd want to get it back. Come on, let's help the boy on his way."

As the two crooks bent over the tangle of bikes John looked over at Sally and winked. But she didn't wink back. She wasn't even looking at him. Slowly, silently she was inching her way toward the outside door.

John suddenly realised that she hadn't been listening at all. She was still planning to make a run for it. It would ruin everything.

"Sally!" he called to her desperately. "Wait a minute!"

It was too late. Sally was already running out the door. The small man turned and saw her. "Bill!" he shouted to his partner. "After her! Quick!"

Bill dropped the bicycle he was holding and raced out the door. John grabbed the small man by the wrist.

"Stay right where you are," he ordered.
"You're under arrest!"

"I'm *what*?"

"Under arrest. I'm a detective so I can do it," said John.

The small man laughed at him and pulled his arm free.
"Don't be stupid, kid," he growled.

Suddenly there were sounds of a scuffle out in the driveway. Sally shouted once and then everything was still again. John groaned. The small man smiled and turned back to him.

18

"Looks like your girlfriend didn't get very far," he said in a low, threatening voice. "Thought you'd try to run away, didn't you? Pretending you were playing along when all the time you were planning a double-cross. Maybe I better tell you something, kid. Nobody double-crosses me and my partner and gets away with it." He took a step toward John.

"Stay right where you are!" barked a voice from the doorway. John and the crook turned to see who had spoken.

A police officer was just coming in the door. A second followed close behind with Bill firmly in tow. Then Sally and the cabby came in and ran to John. The cabby told him everything while the two officers questioned the crooks.

"I drove around the block and when I got back here you weren't anywhere in sight. I thought you might be in trouble so I called in on my radio and the dispatcher got the police. Luckily there was a cruiser only a block away. They got here just in time to catch that big guy chasing Sally." The cabby pointed to Bill, who was shaking his head at the two officers.

John pointed to the pile of bikes. "We were right about those two being the crooks," he said.

"You sure were," replied the cabby. "They have an awful lot of bikes stashed down here. Say, look over there. That one looks just like my son's."

John and Sally helped him pull the bicycle free from the others. The police looked on with interest as the cabby checked it over. The big man swore. The smaller one just glared.

"Now what's all this about stolen bicycles?" one of the officers asked. He made notes while John and Sally explained everything to him.

Later some reporters came and Sally and John explained it all over again for them. The next day the paper had the whole story. *B.A.D. Kids Make Good* read the headline. There was even a picture of all four detectives with the cabby.

"This is just the beginning," John told them all when they met to admire their picture. "The Barton Avenue Detectives are off and rolling. Nothing can stop us now. The crooks in this city better watch their step from now on — everyone knows that the Kids from B.A.D. always get their man."

Allen Morgan
Illustrated by *Andrew Reid*

Mr Wobblegoose's Bicycle

Old Mister Wobblegoose,
nearly ninety-two,
bought himself a bicycle and
didn't know what to do.

Putting on the front brake,
Without due care,
He quickly left the saddle and
went sailing through the air.

Don't be a
WOBBLEGOOSE

★ Make sure that your bike is the right size.

If it's too large, you can't stop and start easily. You're not in control of the bike.

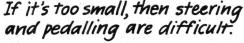

If it's too small, then steering and pedalling are difficult.

★ Are your brakes working properly?

★ Are the tyres in good condition?

★ Is your saddle wobbling?

★ Make sure that you can sit on the saddle and touch the ground with the top half of your foot.

You can? Right... all set!

24

BE SAFE

Did you know that ...

... in two-thirds of cycle accidents for children under 15, children are not taking enough care, and that causes the accident?

So... Keep looking and listening when you're riding your bike.

... the most common type of accident is when cyclists turn right into a side road and hit vehicles coming towards them or from behind them?

So... Be careful when you're on the roads. Make sure you always look in front of you and behind when turning.

NATIONAL CYCLING PROFICIENCY

When you're nine, you can take your Cycling Proficiency Test. Just contact your local road safety officer and you can find out all about it.

Wheeling thro

About 1800 France
These first "bicycles" have wooden wheels and a wooden frame. No steering wheel or pedals.

1870s England
The word "bicycle" becomes common and the "penny-farthing" bicycles are popular. The first tricycles are built and chains are used.

1860s France
The "boneshaker". Clubs are formed and races are held.

1880s England
The first tandems are built and J.B. Dunlop makes tyres filled with air.

ugh time...

1816 Germany
Iron hoops are fitted to the wooden wheels. Still no pedals!

1819 England
Hobby horses are all the rage!

1839 Scotland
The first pedals are added.

1920s
Lightweight bicycles, like the ones we know today, are built.

BIKES TODAY!

The New House Villain

When Mr and Mrs Robinson and Julia saw their new house they all said the same thing.

"Look at that tree."

The tree looked bigger than the house.

"Goodness, we could almost live in the tree," Mrs Robinson cried.

"I think someone is living there already," said Julia. "Some villain or tree pirate!"

While her mother and father were looking at the bathroom and saying they would need new shower curtains, Julia ran outside and looked up into the green and branching tree.

"I know you're there," she called. "Where are you then?"

The Villain looked down out of the tree at her.

He had whiskers that looked like green and brown leaves, and fierce eyes suitable for a Villain.

"Are you coming to live here?" he asked.

"Yes," Julia said. "This is our first visit."

"I shall get out my Villain's Book," said the Villain. "It is called *The Villain's Encyclopaedia of Grips, Tortures and General Wickedness*. Then when you come here I will be able to practise on you." He tried to laugh in a villainous fashion, but the laugh went a bit wrong.

"That wasn't very good," Julia said. "Have another go."

"I wasn't trying very hard," replied the Villain in a snappy voice. He went back among the leaves.

Julia went inside again.

"It's a good house for sunshine," her mother was saying. "It's a pity about that tree though. It must cut off quite a lot of sunshine from the little bedroom, particularly in the winter when you need it most."

"There's a Villain living in that tree," Julia said.

"Is there, dear? Well, don't worry about it too much," her mother replied. "We may have to do something about the tree."

"He's looking up his book of grips and tortures to try on me," said Julia.

"We won't let him hurt you," said her father in a not-listening voice.

"Well," thought Julia, "as though just ordinary parents could do much to protect me from a Villain in a tree. They don't realise that I shall have to be watching every single minute of the day."

She went outside again, back to the tree.

"So there you are," the Villain cried, looking down through the leaves at her. "Feeling pretty scared I expect. Well, just you wait until you see what I've planned for you. If I was to even mention one of my plans, your hair would fall out from sheer terror."

"I've got some plans too," Julia shouted back. "I'm the toughest one in my class at school. I'm tougher than the boys and I know better words. I can bite an iron bar in half with a single crunch."

"I can set things on fire with my mere burning glance," the Villain yelled. "I can knock over a grizzly bear with a single punch."

"A single crunch!" shouted Julia.

"A single punch!" yelled the Villain.

"Even my teacher at school is scared of me," Julia told the tree. "He's three metres high, my teacher, with red glittering eyes and he's covered in long black hair, but he's terrified of me, because I could throw him through the window with a mere toss."

The Villain went back into his Villain nest.

31

Julia went back inside.

They both had something to think about.

Julia's mother had made a cup of tea in the strange, new, empty-looking kitchen. The plastic picnic cups, that looked all right on the beach or in the grass, looked funny on a proper kitchen bench.

"The Villain says he can set things on fire with a single burning glance," Julia told them. "He says he can kill a grizzly bear with a single punch."

"Well, he won't be bothering us for long," said Julia's mother. "That tree shades your bedroom. We've decided to have it cut down. To let the sun in a little more."

"You'd like a bit more sun, wouldn't you?" asked her father. "And it would get rid of that Villain you've been telling us about."

Julia sighed.

"You can get sick from too much sun," she mumbled, but her parents began talking about airing cupboards.

Julia went back to the tree again. The Villain looked down at her.

"So there you are," he said. "Shaking with fright by now, I suppose."

"Well, I've got something for you to think about," said Julia. "My mother and father say they might have your tree cut down."

"What!" yelled the Villain. His beard went all bristly for a moment and then began to wilt. "Why would they cut down such a good tree?"

"To let more sun in," Julia explained.

"Sun!" cried the Villain. "People can get ill from too much sun. Do they know that?"

"I told them," Julia sighed.

The Villain sighed too.

"I shall have to come down from the tree," he said.

The Villain was not very tall. He came up to Julia's shoulder. He wore a big black hat with purple and orange feathers on it.

"Hello," he said.

"You're not very tall," Julia remarked.

"Well, some are and some aren't," the Villain replied in a very stuffy voice. "That's why I need a tree."

They sat beneath the tree thinking hard. At last the Villain spoke.

"First of all you must tell them that the tree gives character to the house. People like a house to have character."

"OK," Julia said.

"And then," the Villain went on, "you must tell them that the sunlight will be more interesting if it comes into the window through a few leaves. Say that you like leaves around your window."

"I can remember that," Julia agreed.

"Say it's a *native* tree," the Villain added. "People think twice before they cut down a native tree."

"Shall I say you need it for extra height?" asked Julia.

"Oh, I wouldn't mention that at all," replied the Villain. "People have no sympathy for Villains. They prefer them small and weak. They don't realise how a bit of danger brightens things up. And how would you know who the good people were if you didn't have the bad people to compare them with? We Villains do a lot of good in a quiet way. But nobody ever thanks us. It would be a dull world if everyone was virtuous."

Julia went inside again.

Her mother and father were packing the cups.

"We're on our way now," her father said, "but we'll be back. How do you like our new house, Julia?"

"The house is all right for a house," Julia answered, "but what about that tree?"

"Well, what about it?" said her father, looking surprised.

"I don't need much sun," Julia cried. "I like the freckly way sun looks when it comes in through a lot of leaves."

"Do you mean that you want us to keep the tree?" asked her mother, looking surprised too.

"It's a native," Julia said. "It adds a lot of character to the house."

"I suppose it does really," her mother said thoughtfully.

"And a tree is a tree after all," said her father, "especially if it's a native tree. But what about that Villain?"

"Oh, I can manage a Villain!" cried Julia. "When I've beaten him, then he'll let me up into the tree and we can do a lot of useful things together. And a Villain stops things from getting dull. How do I know if I'm being good without some Villain to compare myself with?"

"Well, if you want the tree so much we'll leave it," declared Julia's father. "Keeping the Villain in order will be your job."

When Julia went out the Villain was back in the tree again.

"They say they will keep the tree," Julia told him.

"Of course they will," the Villain cried. "I wasn't really worried. You're the one that should worry because I can wrestle a mad gorilla very easily. I'm not tall, but I'm very strong and wicked."

"Well, that's OK," shouted Julia, "because I can pull such horrible faces that gorillas get giddy when they see me. They get giddy and have to sit down with damp flannels on their foreheads. But I've got to go now. I'll be back."

"You'll be sorry," was the Villain's last cry. "You'll be sorry you ever set eyes upon this tree."

But as Julia looked out of the back window of the car she saw him, shaking the thin top branches, tossing and singing high in the tree, very pleased with himself.

"Well, things won't be dull at that house," Julia said to herself. "There's nothing like a Villain to keep things interesting . . ."

And she practised terrible faces all the way home.

Margaret Mahy
Illustrated by *Peter Solomon*

And here's another villain.

BRIAN

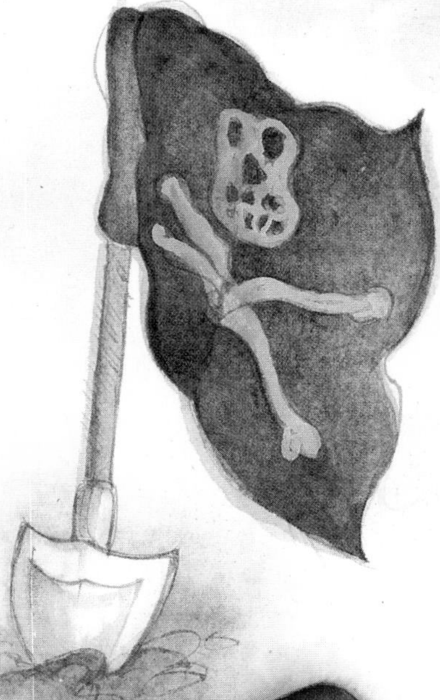

Brian is a baddie,
As nasty as they come.
He terrifies his daddy
And mortifies his mum.

One morning in December
They took him to the zoo,
But Brian lost his temper
And kicked a kangaroo.

And then he fought a lion
Escaping from its pit.
It tried to swallow Brian
Till Brian swallowed it!

Yes, Brian is a devil,
A horrid little curse —
Unlike his brother Neville
Who's infinitely worse!

Doug MacLeod

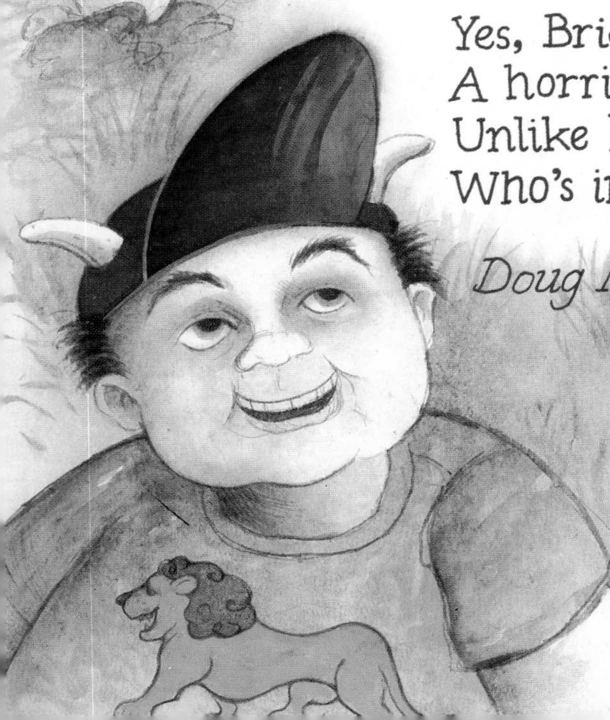

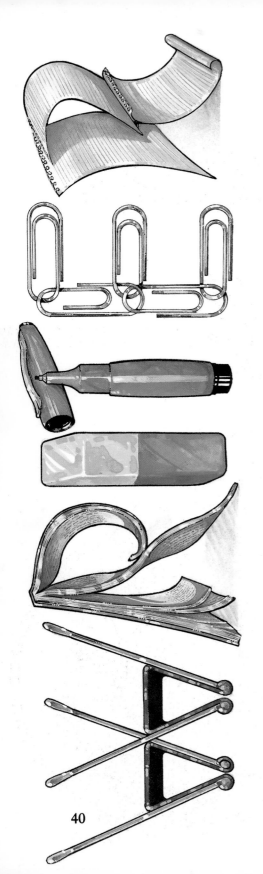

Meet

Name: _Margaret Mahy._

Born at: _Whakatane, New Zealand._

Born on: _21st March, 1936._

Started school at: _Whakatane Infant School._

Favourite subjects at school: _English, reading and composition._

What I didn't like about school: _Having to stop talking._

Favourite food when young: _Scrambled eggs._

Favourite food now: _Wonderful, fried fish._

Best - loved story or book when young: _"The Tale of Mr Tod" by Beatrix Potter._

Favourite kind of books now: _"Labyrinths" by Jorge Luis Borges (adults). "The Iron Man" by Ted Hughes (children)._

Three things I love: _Cats, astronomy. Reading and eating at the same time._

Margaret Mahy

Three things I hate: _Most television advertisements, arguments, ironing._

Secret wish: _A garden with peacocks and an observatory._

Favourite riddle: _What comes out of the forest on sixteen legs? Snow White and the Seven Dwarfs._

Margaret Mahy invented me!

It's my home
NEWCASTLE
upon
TYNE

My city is built on the banks of the River Tyne.

The city got its name from a wooden fort built in the eleventh century. It was called the 'New Castle'. The Castle Keep, which was built between 1172 and 1177, now stands on that site. It cost £911 to build – quite a bargain!

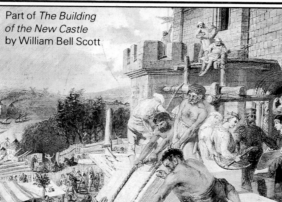

Part of *The Building of the New Castle* by William Bell Scott

In the Middle Ages, Newcastle was a busy market town. People bought and sold wool, cloth, fish, and animal hides. Today Newcastle still has markets. This one takes place every Sunday morning on the Quayside. Lots of people, lots of stalls and lots to buy!

By the sixteenth century, coal mining was much more important to the city than the trade in wool. Coal was sent to different places by ship.

Other industries started to grow in the nineteenth century, such as building ships and steam locomotives. Sir William Armstrong was an engineer and inventor who lived in Newcastle. One of the things he designed and built was the Swing Bridge. It was opened in 1876. It swung open to let the ships go through to the shipyards. Not many go through today.

Out and about in Newcastle

There is lots to see and lots to do in Newcastle. Travel on our Metro and you can see it all! It takes you all around the city and to the seaside as well.

How about...

Try one of our stottie cakes. They're flat breadcakes, about 5cm thick and the size of a frying pan.

Once a year, in June, the Hoppings festival comes to Newcastle. It's the biggest fair in Europe and lots of people come along.

Watching football at St James' Park, Newcastle's home ground.

Going to see the ship models at the Trinity Maritime Centre.

Watching a play at the New Tyne Theatre – it's still got all the special effects, like trapdoors and cannonball thunder.

What's up, Sir Edmund?

How would you like to be one of the people in the photograph on the opposite page? They are climbing Mount Everest, the world's highest mountain.

Mount Everest is in the Himalayas, on the border between Tibet and Nepal. It is 8854 metres high—that's over six times as high as Ben Nevis in Scotland. The first people to climb Mount Everest were Edmund Hillary and his companion Tenzing Norgay who was from Tibet.

Edmund Hillary was born on 20th July 1919 in New Zealand's South Island. He grew up close to the Southern Alps of New Zealand and, as soon as he was old enough, he became a mountaineer.

When he left school, he worked as a bee-keeper, but Edmund continued to climb mountains. He was one of the three people who first climbed the difficult South Ridge on Mount Cook, which is New Zealand's highest mountain (3764 metres high).

In 1953 he joined a British expedition to the Himalayan Mountains. Their plan was to climb to the top of Mount Everest. No-one had ever managed to get to the top, but many had died trying .

At 11.30 am on 29th May 1953, Edmund Hillary and Tenzing Norgay became the first men to "stand on the roof of the world!" They had reached the summit of Mount Everest.

Edmund Hillary was knighted by the Queen, so he became Sir Edmund Hillary. He has led many other expeditions, in the Himalayas and in Antarctica.

SUPERCHOPPERS

This is the tale of Mr Finn
Who couldn't keep his false teeth in.
If he grinned, or if he laughed
Out came his teeth and he looked daft.

If he ate a plate of chips,
He was soon chewing with his lips.
His teeth just lay there on the plate,
Watching him and what he ate.

If he tried to yell or shout,
They would suddenly jump right out,
Go up high into the air
And then sit grinning on his hair.

One day with a cough like croup
They shot right out and looped the loop.
They flew north, then west, then south
And came back tamely to his mouth.

Finn took his dog into the park.
It ran away and with a bark
It chased a child right up a tree.
The child screamed out in misery.

Out shot the teeth hot on the trail
And gripped the bad dog by the tail,
They slowly dragged the beast away
And nipped it hard to make it stay.

After that the dog was good
When they went walking in the wood,
It never even chased a bird.
Trained by teeth: it sounds absurd!

Mr Finn taught in a school,
And there were days he felt a fool,
For every time his teeth popped out
The children would all laugh and shout.

Then one day a girl called Claire
Hid them underneath her chair.
But she wasn't very pleased
When they jumped up and bit her knees!

After that the class was quiet
Or they became the false teeth's diet.
And any children who were rude
Soon shut up when they were chewed.

50

Finn became a fishing champ
Who never got his fingers damp,
The teeth just dived and swam about
And came up with a tasty trout.

Then one day these famous choppers
Were rung up by the local coppers.
Could they stop the rise in crime?
It was increasing all the time.

The Chief of Police had a good plan:
His men would hide Finn in a van.
A message on the radio:
He'd cough and off his teeth would go!

Who's this coming down the hill
In a stolen car? It's Burglar Bill.
He's stopping just outside the bank.
He's twenty stone; built like a tank.

He rushes in and waves his gun.
All the people duck or run.
He demands ten thousand pounds in cash.
Then breaks the glass shield with a crash.

The bank staff quickly give it him,
For Bill could tear them limb for limb.
Then out he runs into the street
Into a policeman on his beat.

Bill quickly knocks him to the ground
As the alarm begins to sound.
In the van Finn was alerted.
He coughed and out his false teeth spurted!

They zoomed around the corner quickly
And pulled Bill from his car quite slickly.
He tried to get loose from their grip,
But they gave his neck a terrible nip.

They pulled him slowly to the van
And dumped him in, a frightened man.
The first of many such adventures
For these tough, crime-busting dentures.

54

Then the PM called up Finn. Can
His teeth track down the man
Who's threatening Earth and, even worse,
Who could destroy the Universe?

Finn's teeth zoomed off across the room
Producing a great sonic boom.
They searched America and China
Europe, Africa, Asia Minor.

PM is an abbreviation for Prime Minister

At last deep in a cave they find
A professor with a crazy mind.
Too late! He has set off his rocket!
Have the teeth the power to stop it?

The rocket soars into deep space
Here come the teeth! What a chase!
There's not a second they can lose.
Ah, they've taken out the fuse.

The threat sails harmlessly away.
Finn's false teeth have saved the day.
History's great criminal stoppers.
Super, Super, Superchoppers!

Written by Paul Groves,
illustrated by Edward McLachlan

Pages from the notebook

WHO INVENTED THEM?

The Bicycle
(Very useful for following suspects.) About 200 years old. A Scottish blacksmith, Kirkpatrick Macmillan, came up with the design for the first bike you could pedal, back in the 1830s.
Interesting note!
He rode 112 km in 10 hours on his new invention, but ended up in jail for reckless riding because he knocked down a young lady.

The Magnifying Glass
(For hunting for finger prints and other clues)
Over 6000 years old!
Seems the ancient Chaldeans, who lived in what is now Iran, had simple magnifying lenses.

Early Greeks and Romans had them too.

The Raincoat
(In case it rains while you're following a crook)
Invented by Charles Macintosh (another Scot!) in 1823.

How does it work? The telephone

1   You lift the handpiece. A switch immediately "tells" your local exchange that you want to make a call.

2   The equipment at your local exchange "replies" by sending you "dial tone".

3   You "tell" the exchange what number you want by dialling that number. If your friend lives far away, your exchange will link with other exchanges before connecting you to your friend's phone.

4   When your two phones are connected, the exchange sends a signal along the wire to ring your friend's phone. You are sent a different sound, "ringing tone", to let you know what's happening.

THE TELEPHONE EXCHANGE

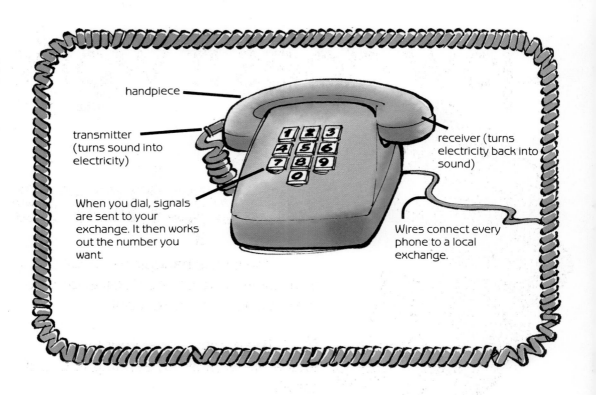

handpiece

transmitter
(turns sound into
electricity)

receiver (turns
electricity back into
sound)

When you dial, signals
are sent to your
exchange. It then works
out the number you
want.

Wires connect every
phone to a local
exchange.

5   When your friend says "hello", she speaks into the
transmitter. It turns her "hello" into electricity.

6   Her "hello" travels as an electric current along the
wires at incredible speed. If you were in Aberdeen and your
friend in Paris, her "hello" would reach you in much less
than a second.

7   When her "hello" reaches your
phone, it is turned back into the sound of
her voice by the receiver.

CATCH A CROOK!

Can you help these detectives catch their crooks?

WORDS TO TRACK DOWN

Glossary

all sewn up (*p. 7*)
solved; finished

basement (*p. 13*)
a room below street level

blocks (*p. 6*)
streets

bristly (*p. 33*)
stiff

cabby (*p. 8*)
taxi-driver

conversationally (*p. 9*)
chattily

croup (*p. 47*)
an illness that babies sometimes get which causes a very noisy cough

cruising (*p. 6*)
driving slowly

cruiser (*p. 20*)
police car

curse (*p. 39*)
something bad

dentures (*p. 54*)
false teeth

desperately (*p. 17*)
wildly; with concern

discussion (*p. 16*)
talk

dispatcher (*p. 20*)
person who tells the taxi drivers where to go to pick up passengers

double-cross (*p. 19*)
to cheat by pretending

figured (*p. 7*)
thought

giddy (*p. 37*)
to get dizzy

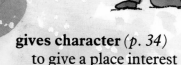

gives character (*p. 34*)
to give a place interest

hide (*p. 42*)
the skin of an animal

inching (*p. 17*)
moving very slowly

infinitely worse (*p. 39*)
much, much worse

investigate (*p. 13*)
search; find out

Glossary continues on page 64

mere *(p. 31)*
only

meter *(p. 8)*
a machine that measures
how much you've used

mortifies *(p. 39)*
to make someone feel
upset or ashamed

off and rolling *(p. 21)*
they are successful and will
carry on being so

pursuit *(p. 6)*
to follow or chase

registration number *(p. 6)*
number plate

relieved *(p. 17)*
stopped worrying

scuffle *(p. 18)*
fight

shrugged *(p. 8)*
shrug your shoulders –
to show you're not
bothered

sit tight *(p. 16)*
to stay where you are

slickly *(p. 54)*
very smoothly and quickly

sonic boom *(p. 54)*
a sound like an explosion
made by an aircraft
travelling faster than the
speed of sound

stashed *(p. 20)*
hidden; stored

studied *(p. 12)*
looked closely

stuffy *(p. 34)*
snobby

suspicious *(p. 11)*
guessing that something
is wrong

sympathy *(p. 34)*
feeling sorry for

triumphantly *(p. 14)*
full of joy because
you're successful

villainous fashion *(p. 29)*
in an evil way

virtuous *(p. 34)*
to be good all the time

wilt *(p. 33)*
to droop (flowers start
to wilt)